People of the Bible

The Bible through stories and pictures

Jesus Begins His Work

Jesus Begins His Work

Retold by Catherine Storr
Pictures by Chris Molan

Methuen Children's Books
in association with Belitha Press Ltd

Every year Mary and Joseph used to go
to Jerusalem for the feast of the Passover.
When Jesus was twelve years old,
he went with them.

When the feasting was over,
Mary and Joseph started
on the long journey back to Nazareth.
Jesus wasn't with them.

They thought he was travelling
with some other friends and relations.
It wasn't until the end of the first day
that they discovered he had been left behind.

Joseph and Mary had to go back to Jerusalem.
They looked everywhere for Jesus.
At last they found him in the Temple.
He was talking to the clever men there,
asking questions, and answering them too.

Mary said to him,
'How could you do this to us?
We've been terribly worried about you.'
Jesus said, 'Don't you know I have to do
what God tells me?'
But he went back to Nazareth with Joseph and Mary
and did what he was told.

Many years later, John the Baptist, a cousin of Jesus, was living in the wilderness.
He taught people to share their clothes and food with others, who were cold and hungry.
He said to them, 'I am not the greatest prophet.
But he is coming soon.
I have seen him and I know he is the son of God.'

One day, John was with two of his followers, Andrew and Simon Peter.
He saw Jesus coming and he said to them, 'Look! There is the son of God.'

When Andrew heard this,
he left John and followed Jesus.
He said to his brother, Simon Peter,
'Come and see. We have found Christ, our leader.'
Jesus said, 'Follow me!'

Soon after this Jesus found Philip,
who followed him too.
As well as Andrew and Simon Peter and Philip,
there were James and John the sons of Zebedee,
Matthew and Bartholomew, Thomas and Simon,
James the son of Alphaeus, Thaddeus,
and Judas Iscariot.
All these men were called the disciples of Jesus.

One day there was a great wedding party
in a village called Cana.
Mary and Jesus and his disciples had all been invited.

But when they arrived at the feast,
all the wine had been drunk.

Mary said to Jesus, 'There's no more wine
for the guests to drink. Is there anything you can do?'
She said to the servants,
'Whatever my son tells you, you should do.'

Jesus told the servants to fill six great jars with water.
Then he said, 'Pour something to drink from the jars,
and take it to the master of the house.'
As they did this,
they saw that the water had turned into wine.
It was even better wine than they had drunk before.
This was Jesus' first miracle.

After this Jesus did many more miracles.
He made ill people better.
Once he was teaching in a house full of people,
and a man who couldn't stand or walk
was lowered on his bed through the roof
into the middle of the house.
Jesus said to him, 'Take up your bed and walk.'
The man found that he could do as he was told.
He was cured.

Another time, a blind man was brought to Jesus.
Jesus spat on some earth and rubbed it
on the man's eyes. Then he asked,
'What do you see?' The man said,
'I see men, like trees, but walking.'
He could see again.

One day, a ruler of the synagogue,
called Jairus, came to see Jesus and said,
'My little daughter is dying. Please save her.'
Jesus went to Jairus' house and found everyone there
crying and wailing. He said, 'Don't be sad.
The little girl isn't dead, she's only asleep.'
He went inside and took her by the hand and said,
'Get up!'
The little girl stood up, alive and well. Jesus said,
'Give her some food, and let's keep it a secret.'

Jesus and his disciples travelled to many places.
They took no money or food,
and taught people who came to listen to them.

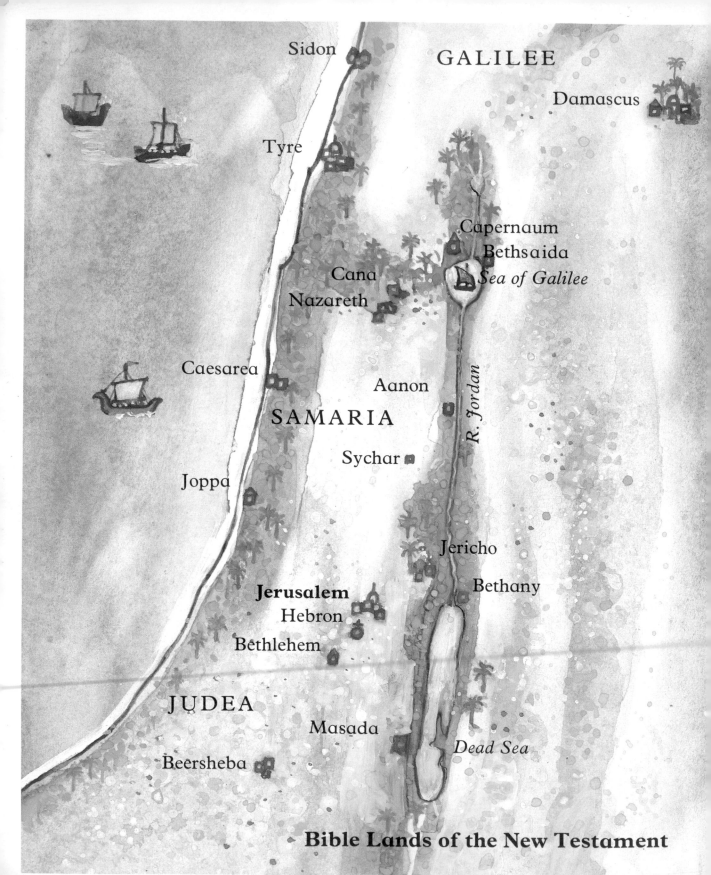

Sidon

GALILEE

Damascus

Tyre

Capernaum
Bethsaida
Sea of Galilee

Cana
Nazareth

Caesarea

Aanon

R. Jordan

SAMARIA

Sychar

Joppa

Jericho

Bethany

Jerusalem
Hebron

Bethlehem

JUDEA

Masada

Dead Sea

Beersheba

Bible Lands of the New Testament

First published 2000 in *The Macmillan Treasury of Nursery Stories*
This collection first published 2010 by Macmillan Children's Books
a division of Macmillan Publishers Limited
20 New Wharf Road, London N1 9RR
Basingstoke and Oxford
Associated companies throughout the world
www.panmacmillan.com

ISBN: 978-0-230-74993-1

A CIP catalogue record for this book is available from the British Library.

Printed in China

MACMILLAN CHILDREN'S BOOKS

Beauty and the Beast
and other stories

Retold by
Mary Hoffman

Illustrated by
Anna Currey

Beauty and the Beast

There was once a rich merchant who had six children: three sons and three daughters. He happily spent his money on their education and they all had fine clothes and valuable ornaments and jewellery. They were all good-looking young people, but the youngest daughter was the most attractive of all of them. When she was small, she was known as "the little beauty" and the name stuck. She had no name but Beauty.

This did not make her popular with her two sisters, who were not very nice-natured. They were jealous of

Beauty, who was as kind and sweet as she was pretty. The older sisters were very vain and proud and wouldn't have anything to do with the other merchants' daughters.

They were often courted by young men, since they were handsome, but they always said, "Oh, no, we wouldn't marry anyone lower than a Duke!" Beauty had her admirers, too, but she just said, "Thank you, but I am too young to marry. I want to stay with my father a few years more."

Then disaster struck. The merchant's ships were all lost at sea, with all his goods upon them. He had to sell his fine house in town and his carriage and retire to a small farm he owned in the country. The merchant and his sons now worked long hours on their land and there was no money for luxuries.

It took Beauty a few weeks to adjust to her new life. She didn't miss the balls and the dancing and the fine dresses, but it was hard to get up at four every morning and light the fires and cook the food for the family. But Beauty did all this and grew strong, while her sisters stayed

in bed till ten o'clock and spent the whole day lamenting their loss of fortune.

Then, one day, a message reached the merchant that one of his ships had survived and was coming into a nearby port. The old man's heart leapt to think that he might recover some of his money and perhaps relieve Beauty of some of her household burdens. His two oldest daughters thought only of regaining their finery and asked him to bring back ever so many trinkets and fripperies from the town.

"What about you, Beauty?" asked her father. "Is there nothing you would like?"

Beauty thought hard, because she didn't want her father to spend any of his regained money on frivolities. "I should like a rose, Father," she said at last, thinking she was asking for something simple

and little knowing how much trouble it would cause.

Well, the merchant rode to the port and his ship had indeed returned, but his debts were so great that he had to sell everything on board it to pay for them. There was nothing left over for even a scrap of lace for a flighty daughter. He was a bitter man as he rode back home after his wasted journey.

But his problems increased as the weather worsened. First, the rain came down and then there was thunder and lightning. The merchant's clothes were drenched and his horse was a sorry sight. They were in the middle of a wild wood, lashed by wind and rain.

Just when he thought he couldn't bear any more discomfort, the merchant saw a light through the trees. He urged his horse towards it, and found a splendid castle, all illuminated but with no sign of life in it.

The horse found his way to a stable and tucked in

eagerly to the hay and oats he found there. The merchant rubbed him down with some straw and tied him to the manger.

Then he entered the castle itself, calling out as he went but seeing no one. The merchant's wet footsteps squelched on the thick carpets as he made his way from room to room.

He found a dining-room, with a table laid for one, and went over to the roaring fire in the grate. He was soon warm and reasonably dry, but very hungry.

At last, at about eleven o'clock, the merchant could bear it no longer. He ate the cold roast chicken and drank a glass or two of wine. Then he felt very sleepy and wandered off to find a bedroom. No sooner did he spy a comfortable-looking bed, than he fell on it and into a deep sleep.

When he woke, refreshed, the next morning, the merchant was astonished to find his weather-stained

clothes removed and a new suit in his size laid out for him. "This castle must belong to a kind fairy!" he exclaimed. He went hopefully back to the dining-room and found hot chocolate and a good breakfast waiting for him.

"Thank you, kind fairy," he said, as he went out to the stable to collect his horse. He was leading him out through the gardens, when he noticed a splendid rose-bush and remembered Beauty. "I may not have anything for my other daughters," he thought, "but I could at least take Beauty her rose." And he broke a branch off the bush.

All of a sudden, there was a terrifying growling and a monstrous beast came through the garden.

"Ungrateful wretch!" he roared. "I have fed you and housed you and given you fresh garments and this is how you repay me, by stealing my roses, which are more precious to me than anything else. For this you will die!"

And the beast made as if to devour the merchant on the spot. The poor man fell to his knees and begged for mercy. "Forgive me, my lord. I had no idea they meant so much to you. I was only going to take some roses for my youngest daughter, Beauty."

"Talk not to me of daughters!" growled the beast. "Nor call me 'my lord'. My name is Beast, and I tell you, I shall eat you for your impertinence. But I am willing to wait three months. Give me your word that you will return here then, if one of your children does not volunteer to take your place."

"I promise, my . . . Beast," said the merchant, thinking that at least he would see his children again before he died. Then the Beast seemed to relent a bit. "Before you go," he said, "you may return to your room and put in a chest that you will find there anything  you will find there anything you want to take. It will be sent on to you. I am not an ungenerous host; I just can't

bear people taking my roses."

So the merchant went back and packed the chest with large gold pieces that he found in his room. He wept as  he did so, thinking that he would be able to lighten his children's poverty, though at a terrible cost.

He travelled home with a heavy heart, but took comfort from the welcome his children gave him, especially Beauty. He gave her the branch of roses, but could not help saying as he did so, "Here are your roses, but I am likely to pay for them with my life."

Then his children wouldn't rest till they had got the whole story out of him. "Huh!" said his oldest daughter. "Typical of Beauty!"

"Yes," said the other. "Look how she doesn't even shed a tear for her father's life!"

"That is because I know he will not have to give it," said Beauty, calmly. "It was my fault that the Beast was enraged, so I shall go in my father's place."

Her brothers said they couldn't allow it, that they would go with weapons and kill the Beast, but Beauty said she would not dream of endangering their lives. Her father

said he had only a few years left to live and it was better for him to die than one so young and lovely with her life before her. But Beauty was not persuaded. She told her father that he could not stop her from accompanying him in three months' time. Her sisters didn't attempt to dissuade her at all; they were quite pleased at the idea of getting rid of her.

The next morning, the merchant was amazed to find the chest of gold pieces by his bed. He told no one about it but Beauty, who said, "Father, while you were away, two suitors came asking for my sisters in marriage. Do use some of this money for their dowries."

"I believe you are right, Beauty. It would give me great comfort to know that they were settled in life, before I keep my promise to the Beast," said the merchant, who could still not accept that Beauty was going to stand in for him.

But when it was time for him to return to the Beast's castle, Beauty saddled her own little pony and rode beside him. Her sisters had to rub their eyes with an onion to feign tears, but her brothers were genuinely sad to see her go.

When they arrived at the castle, the horses took themselves to the stable and the merchant led Beauty to the dining-room. There were two places laid and the merchant, knowing a little more of how the castle worked this time, urged Beauty to sit and eat. Neither of them had much of an appetite.

After supper, they heard the growling noise which meant that the Beast was approaching. Brave as she was, Beauty's heart quaked within her. And when she saw him, she was almost faint with terror. But the Beast was very courteous and polite. Even at the last minute, Beauty's father tried to persuade her to change her mind, but she was quite resolute.

She said goodbye to her father with many tears and the Beast withdrew. Alone in the castle, Beauty found a door with "BEAUTY'S CHAMBER" written above it. Inside was a beautiful room, all fitted out with the finest silks and satins and a large four-poster bed. There were books to read and painting materials and a harpsichord.

"Would the Beast really have gone to so much trouble if he meant to eat me straightaway?" thought Beauty. She went to bed and, in spite of her situation, slept well.

In the morning, servants brought her gorgeous dresses to choose from, all made specially to her size and, again, Beauty thought that this would not have been done if she were to die soon. She passed a pleasant day in her comfortable room and wandering through the castle's beautiful gardens.

At supper time, she heard the Beast coming and had to screw up all her courage to face him. But he merely asked if he might sit with her while she ate, and she could hardly object.

"Do you find me very ugly?" asked the Beast, and Beauty found it difficult to answer. She didn't want to hurt his feelings.

"Perhaps you are somewhat ugly in appearance," she said, "but you seem to be kind and you have exquisite manners."

The Beast was pleased with her answer. And so a pattern developed to their days. Beauty played her harpsichord and painted pictures and read books and went for long walks. Anything she wanted appeared magically before her. Indeed, when she wished to know how her father was, the looking-glass in her room immediately  showed her a picture of him returning home.

Over the weeks, she saw in the mirror that her sisters were married and that her father and brothers were still sad about her absence. She had no more fears about being eaten by the Beast. She saw him only at supper time, but came to look forward to his visits. It was the only company she had and she enjoyed their conversations.

The only thing that troubled her was that the Beast asked her to marry him. She said no, but he repeated his request every evening. It distressed her to upset him, but she said, "Dear Beast, you know I am very fond of you and I know you have a kind heart and a good nature. But I can never marry you."

One night, when he had received his answer, the Beast said, "If you will not marry me, Beauty, promise me this —that you will never leave me."

Beauty thought about it. She was really happy at the castle and wanted for nothing and she had become really very used to the Beast and fond of him.

"I will promise you that," said Beauty, "if you will let me have one visit home first to see my father and family again."

"I can deny you nothing," said the Beast, "but you must return after a week, or I shall die of grief. Just place this ring on your bedside table when you want to return."

Next morning, when Beauty awoke, she found to her delight that she was in her father's house. How the maid screamed when she entered the room to clean it! Beauty's father and brothers were overjoyed to see her. They sent for her sisters, who came with their husbands. But Beauty was sad to see that they were not as happy and contented as she was.

The first one had married a very handsome man, but he was so vain and selfish that he didn't really care about anyone but himself. The second had married a very agreeable and witty man but, after their marriage, he used his wit at her expense and was very sarcastic and cruel.

The sisters were green with jealousy to see Beauty's fine clothes and to observe how well she looked and to

hear how happy she was with the Beast. Secretly, they plotted to keep her longer than a week. "Perhaps then he will be angry and come and eat her after all," they said.

So, when the week was up, they pretended they couldn't do without Beauty and persuaded her to stay a few days. She was worried about the Beast, but didn't like to upset her sisters, who were not usually so nice to her.

But, after a few days, she had a terrible dream. The Beast was lying in his rose garden, looking as if he might be dead.

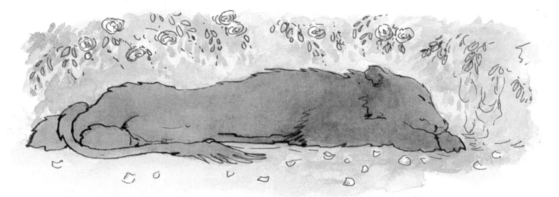

"Oh, no!" thought Beauty. "What have I done?"

She immediately put the ring on her bedside table and was transported back to her chamber in the Beast's castle. She had never known where he spent his days and, though she searched the castle, she could not find him. Impatiently, she waited for supper time, and could not eat a thing because she expected the Beast at any minute. But he did not come.

Desperate, she rushed out into the grounds and,

remembering her dream, ran to the rose garden. And there he was, lying on the ground as if dead.

"Oh, it is all my fault!" cried Beauty, running to his side. She covered his hairy ugly face with kisses and wept over him. "Oh, my poor Beast, do not die! I should never forgive myself. Only live and I will marry you. For what do looks matter beside a kind and gentle heart?"

The Beast opened his eyes and—he was not a beast any more! Beauty found herself embracing a handsome young man. She jumped up in confusion. "Where is the Beast?" she cried.

"Here, Beauty," said the young man. "I was under an enchantment put upon me by a wicked fairy. I had to remain a beast until a beautiful young woman freely offered to marry me. You have saved me from the spell."

The two were happy as could be and Beauty's family were all brought to the castle in an instant. Beauty and her prince were married with great splendour, but her two sisters were turned into statues which had to stand at the gates, watching the young couple living happily, until their bad natures had turned to good. And I don't suppose that happened at all soon.

The Little Red Hen

Once upon a time a little red hen set up house with a cat, a dog and a pig. She was very hard working and did all the cooking and cleaning. The others were terribly lazy and didn't do anything they didn't have to.

One day, the little red hen thought it would be nice to have home-made bread. Her friends thought it was a good idea, too, so the little red hen started right at the beginning and bought some wheat.

"Now, who will help me plant the wheat?" she asked.

The cat said, "I won't."

The dog said, "I won't."

The pig said, "I won't,
I won't, I won't."

"All right, then," said
the little red hen. "I'll just
have to do it myself." And she
planted all the wheat seeds herself.

Next she asked, "Who will help me water the wheat?"

The cat said, "I won't."

The dog said, "I won't."

The pig said, "I won't, I won't, I won't."

"All right, then," said the little red hen. "I'll just have to
do it myself." And she watered the
wheat every day.

Eventually it was
harvest-time, and
the little red hen
asked, "Who will help
me cut the wheat?"

The cat said, "I won't."

The dog said, "I won't."

The pig said, "I won't, I won't, I won't."

"All right, then," said the little red hen. "I'll just have to do it myself." And she took a little scythe and harvested all the wheat.

Now it was time to grind the wheat to make flour. So the little red hen asked, "Who will help me take the sacks of wheat to the miller to be ground?"

The cat said, "I won't."

The dog said, "I won't."

The pig said, "I won't, I won't, I won't."

"All right, then," said the little red hen. "I'll just have to do it myself." And she got the farmer to take her to the miller's and back on his cart.

Now that she had the flour, the little red hen could make the first loaf.

"Who will help me make the bread?" she asked.

The cat said, "I won't."

The dog said, "I won't."

The pig said, "I won't, I won't, I won't."

"All right, then," said the little red hen. "I'll just have to do it myself." And she mixed the dough, kneaded it and left it to rise.

Some hours later, she asked, "Who will help me bake the bread?"

The cat said, "I won't."

The dog said, "I won't."

The pig said, "I won't, I won't, I won't."

"All right, then," said the little red hen. "I'll just have to do it myself." And she put the bread in the oven, watched over it to make sure it didn't burn, then took it out to cool when it was done.

A delicious smell of freshly baked bread filled the kitchen and the friends gathered round.

"Now," said the little red hen. "Who will help me eat the bread?"

The cat said, "I will!"

The dog said, "I will!"

The pig said, "I will, I will, I will!"

"All right, then," yawned the little red hen. "But you'll have to help yourselves. I'm going to sit down for a while. There's butter and strawberry jam in the larder."

And the little red hen sat down in the armchair and fell fast asleep. The three friends looked at one another and were ashamed. They knew they had done nothing towards making the bread.

The cat fetched a pillow and put it under the little red hen's head. The dog washed up all the cooking things. The pig made a big pot of tea for all of them and cut slices of the bread and spread it thickly with butter and jam.

When the little red hen woke up from her doze, she found the house clean and tidy and a tray on the table beside her with a mug of tea and a plate of bread and jam. She was very surprised.

"How kind you all are," she said. "You are the best friends in the world!"

And the cat, the dog and the pig all privately vowed that, from then on, they would be.

The Country Mouse and the City Mouse

There were once two mice who were good friends. One was a house mouse who lived in a big city and the other was a field mouse who lived in the countryside.

The city mouse paid his friend a visit in the country and the field mouse was very glad to see him.

"Come with me and we will have a feast of ripe barley

and wheat," he said.

The city mouse ate a good dinner but he didn't seem satisfied.

"Ah," he sighed. "You should see what I get to eat in the town— cheese, figs, honey, sultanas, apples. You would soon tire of all this field-food if you tasted city life. Why don't you come and stay with me so I can show you?"

So the country mouse went home with his friend. He was very frightened by all the many pairs of feet and carriage wheels on the street and very relieved when they reached the city mouse's house.

As soon as the city mouse had shown his friend his comfortable home behind the skirting board, they set out to find their dinner.

"You see how conveniently my home is situated,"

boasted the city mouse. "In the kitchen, the best room in all the house."

He led his friend through a tiny crack at the bottom of a door into a larder, where there were the most delicious smells. The little country mouse's mouth watered. They scampered up onto a high shelf where there sat a tasty cheese. But no sooner had they started to nibble the edges off it than a large person opened the larder door and reached for the shelf!

The mice scuttled away and hid. When all was quiet again they came out and this time climbed onto the kitchen table. In the middle of it was a handsome cake, made with sultanas and cherries and many other kinds of dried fruit. The country mouse's whiskers twitched. This was finer fare than he ever found in a field.

But they had not tasted more than a crumb of the

cake's icing before someone else came into the room and they had to run and hide again. Back in the city mouse's hole, the country mouse gasped for breath, his little heart pounding.

"You can keep your fine city food," he panted. "I grant you it is very fine indeed and probably delicious but you have to put up with so many dangers to get it that, as for me, I would rather eat the humble grains I find in the fields than risk so much to get fancier meals."

And he headed back to the country where he lived happily for the rest of his days, though he never tasted cake. And the city mouse lived happily, too, because he was used to the dangers of his way of life and much too fond of cake to leave it behind.

Sip and her Sisters

Once upon a time there was a king with three daughters. The oldest was called Sip. The next oldest was called Sipsippernip. And the third and youngest daughter was called Sipsippernipsipsirumsip.

In the neighbouring country there was another king who had three sons. The oldest son was called Skrat. The second was called Skratskratterat. And the third and youngest son was called Skratskratteratskratskirumskrat.

One day the first king went to have tea with the other

one and introduced his daughters to the other king's sons.

They got on famously. And in a short while the three princesses were engaged to the three princes.

Their wedding day came and this was how it was:

Sip got Skrat,

Sipsippernip got Skratskratterat,

and Sipsippernipsipsirumsip got Skratskratteratskratskirumskrat.

What do you think of that?